Derrida and the End of History

Stuart Sim

ICON BOOKS UK

TOTEM BOOKS USA

Published in the UK in 1999
by Icon Books Ltd., Grange Road,
Duxford, Cambridge CB2 4QF
email: info@iconbooks.co.uk
www.iconbooks.co.uk

Published in the USA in 1999
by Totem Books
Inquiries to: PO Box 223,
Canal Street Station,
New York, NY 10013

Distributed in the UK, Europe,
Canada, South Africa and Asia
by the Penguin Group:
Penguin Books Ltd.,
27 Wrights Lane,
London W8 5TZ

In the United States,
distributed to the trade by
National Book Network Inc.,
4720 Boston Way, Lanham,
Maryland 20706

Published in Australia in 1999
by Allen & Unwin Pty. Ltd.,
PO Box 8500, 9 Atchison Street,
St. Leonards, NSW 2065

Library of Congress Catalog
Card Number: 99-071120

Reprinted 2000

Series editor: Richard Appignanesi

ISBN 1 84046 094 6

Typesetting by Wayzgoose

Printed and bound in the UK by
Cox & Wyman Ltd., Reading

Questioning History

'How can one be late to the end of history? A question for today.'[1] Jacques Derrida's fame rests largely on his ability to devise eccentric approaches to philosophical and cultural problems, and he might well be thought to have excelled himself with this particular question. Assuming, that is, that one felt 'the end of history' made any sense as a concept, given that, as some thinkers would have it, history is the equivalent of humankind's memory. Thus we have the historian Arthur Marwick inviting us to

try to imagine what everyday life would be like in a society in which no one knew any history. Imagination boggles, because it is only through knowledge of its history that a society can have knowledge of itself. As a man without memory and self-knowledge is a man adrift, so a society without memory (or more correctly, without recollection) and self-knowledge would be a society adrift.[2]

If it *is* a question, then, *why* is it a question? And is it in any way an important question, or just another one of Derrida's notorious conundrums that only succeed in leaving the majority of readers baffled? Derrida has built a reputation out of iconoclasm (famously, and counterintuitively, arguing that writing precedes speech, for example), and we might be inclined to dismiss the question above as just another one of his self-consciously provocative intellectual games; particularly since it is posed in the course of a book called *Specters of Marx* (1993; American translation, hence spelling), in which Derrida tries to resurrect the reputation of Karl Marx at quite possibly the lowest point of that thinker's intellectual history. In the aftermath of the pulling down of the Berlin Wall, the visible proof of the collapse of Soviet communism and its satellite states, that is just about as iconoclastic as one could be; especially if one goes on to propound a reading of Marx that can only alienate those still calling themselves Marxists. Derrida's Marx is, as he puts it, 'plural' – 'there is more than one of them, there must be more than one of them';[3] that is, Marx is open to interpretation and revision in response to changing cultural circumstances, not a source of gospel truth as to how to change the world for the better by the reorganisation of its economic and political life according to universally-applicable principles.

Not only can 'classical' Marxists not accept this reading of Marx – they must regard it as little better than heresy. A 'plural' Marx is, for true believers anyway, a contradiction in terms. Not that true believers are likely to expect too much from anyone who could also say, as Derrida has elsewhere in his extensive *oeuvre*, that there is 'a Marxism of the right and a Marxism of the left'.[4] This is another dangerously heretical notion, from someone seemingly determined to challenge and unsettle received wisdom as much as he possibly can.

So why the question? Derrida is specifically

responding in this instance to the claim made by the American political theorist Francis Fukuyama, in his controversial book *The End of History and the Last Man* (1992), that history has ended because Western liberal democracy has triumphed over communism – and, by implication, over Marxism too. The 'good news' to be announced is that ideological conflict is potentially a thing of the past, now that we have come to realise that 'the ideal of liberal democracy could not be improved upon'.[5] A whole new world order beckons (as the 'good news' phrase suggests, there is an evangelical tone to *The End of History*). Although Fukuyama's bold contention had many adherents in the heady period immediately following communism's collapse in Europe in the 1980s, Derrida is one of what soon became a growing body of dissenting voices suggesting that it was not really that simple after all. '[H]ow is it that a discourse of this type', Derrida queries in his most confrontational tone, *is sought out by those who celebrate the triumph of liberal capitalism and its pre-destined alliance with liberal democracy only in order to hide, and first of all from themselves, the fact that this triumph has never been so critical, fragile, threatened, even in certain regards catastrophic, and in sum bereaved?*[6]

Communism in Europe had disintegrated, yes, but did that necessarily entail that liberal democracy, and its attendant capitalist economic system, had won? More pertinently, did all of us *want* liberal democratic capitalism to win – or even think it desirable that it did so? As the 'Editors' Introduction' to Derrida's *Specters* put it, 'many of us felt a vague sense of foreboding' about the changes likely to come about after the apparent victory of free market economics; a fear that such changes might prove to be at least as 'malign . . . as benign'.[7] The task Derrida sets himself in *Specters* (the fruit of an international colloquium on the future of Marxism, held at the University of California in 1993[8]), is to flesh out what lies behind that sense of foreboding, in order to prove that Fukuyama's claims amount to little more than an ideological confidence trick. For 'end of history' read, in effect, suppression of political opposition by the new powers-that-be.

Fukuyama is not, however, the only one to proclaim the end of history. Many other thinkers in recent years, such as the French postmodernist theorists Jean Baudrillard and Jean-François Lyotard, have contributed to this debate, which itself is part of a much larger debate that goes under the name of 'endism'. In its turn, endism is often considered to be one of the distinguishing features of the postmodern culture that we are constantly being informed we now inhabit. Derrida's question thus has greater significance than might at first appear, and the spirit that lies behind his subsequent response is one with a great deal to commend it. It is a question, Derrida insists, that 'obliges one to wonder if the end of history is but the end of a certain *concept* of history'.[9] Eminently sensible though this sentiment sounds, things are never quite that straightforward with Derrida, and the statement is merely the prelude to a magical mystery tour around both Marx and endism (with digressions to Shakespeare and various other points on the literary and philosophical compass on the way); a tour whose roots lie deep within the philosophical movement known as *deconstruction*. (See 'Key Ideas' at the end of this book.) Why Derrida would be fascinated with the question; why he would be moved to add his voice to the debate; and how important his final contribution to that debate actually proves to be, form the basis for this present inquiry.

Understanding Derrida

Derrida arouses strong emotions, even in those who have never read him but only *heard* about him and deconstruction, the highly controversial school of thought which he has inspired. Witness the by now well-worn joke that the difference between the Mafia and deconstruction is that the former makes you an offer you can't refuse, the latter an offer you can't understand. Lack of understanding has, in fact, dogged Derrida almost from the beginning of his long career: a state of affairs that the almost wilful obscurity of much of his writings has done nothing to dispel. Even his most ardent supporters are forced to acknowledge that he sets us considerable problems of comprehension, with the cultural theorist Christopher Norris, for example, conceding that Derrida's writing style

will strike most philosophers – at least those in the dominant Anglo-American tradition – as a style of extravagant metaphorical whimsy. Such wordplay, they are likely to argue, is at most a kind of sophistical doodling on the margins of serious, truth-seeking discourse.[10]

Critics, predictably enough, are even harsher in their assessment of the value of Derrida's philosophical project, accusing him of everything from an irresponsible pessimism to the attempted destruction of the subject of philosophy itself. As one has put it, in appropriately outraged form, Derrida's form of textual analysis is 'endless, treacherous and terrifying':[11] hardly the traits to recommend a cultural theorist to us in the normal course of events. The reader is therefore entitled to know at this early stage of the proceedings what she is letting herself in for, and whether this promises to be a pro- or an anti-Derrida inquiry. It will be, ultimately, pro-, although not uncritically so (no defence of doodling, treachery or terror, anyway). Not only will it be argued here that Derrida's contribution to the endist debate is culturally extremely important; but also that it provides a way into deconstruction that helps to make it seem a far less esoteric area of intellectual activity than its current reputation amongst the wider public would suggest. Maybe, in this instance, the offer can be understood: that will be our goal, anyway.

Endism

It seems a good idea to start by considering briefly the phenomenon of 'endism'. This is a catchy name for a wide range of positions and thinkers whose common element is that they are announcing 'the end' of something or other – history, humanism, ideology, modernity, philosophy, Marxism, the author, 'man', and the world being amongst the most popular candidates of late. Endism is by no means a new historical phenomenon. Many a religion has forecast the end of the world in the past, often several times over. What gives endist thought a new twist, or at the very least a certain added *frisson*, is the advent of a new millennium. The later 20th century has constituted particularly fertile ground for endist speculation of all kinds – including the development of what Derrida has referred to, somewhat slightingly, as the 'apocalyptic tone in philosophy'.[12] *Fin de siècle* periods traditionally have been highly receptive to such 'apocalyptic' speculation, of course. Significant chronological landmarks do tend to concentrate the mind in this regard.

Many of these ends are connected: when ideology ends, so does history; when modernity ends, so do humanism and Marxism; when our current concept of 'man' ends, so does humanism again. The end of the world, as the Green movement has been warning us for some time, might come about because of the combined excesses of ideology, modernity, humanism and Marxism, which collectively have put the survival of our environment severely at risk. Taking the longer view, some scientists and philosophers invite us to contemplate the apparently inescapable end of our universe a few billion years down the line from now, when our sun is scheduled to burn out, and ask ourselves whether *this* event should not be our primary concern. Lyotard even suggested in late career that this coming cataclysm might be the single biggest problem currently facing us: 'While we talk, the sun is getting older. It will explode in 4.5 billion years. It's just a little beyond the halfway point of its expected life-time. . . . That, in my view, is the sole serious question to face humanity today.'[13] (His solution will be considered below, by the way.)

Endist thinking fits in very neatly with the cultural movement known as postmodernism, which actively encourages us to free ourselves from traditional authority and the hold that the past can exert on our thought and behaviour. French cultural theorists are very much to the fore here. The 'death of man' (often referred to as the 'death of the subject'), as propounded by Michel Foucault, for example, is to be read as the death of a particular conception of man sanctioned by the humanist tradition, in which man is seen to be 'the measure of all things', as well as capable of endless 'improvement' at the personal level. For Foucault, this was an act of presumption on our part that led to a distorted view of human nature, and, as such, an ideal that could well be discarded: 'man is an invention of recent date', he claimed, 'And perhaps one nearing its end'.[14] When that end comes, it need be regarded as having no greater significance than the erasure of 'a face drawn in sand at the edge of the sea'.[15] Claude Lévi-Strauss had earlier voiced similar sentiments in his anthropological studies, which tended to play down the significance of individuals (or 'subjects') in the scheme of things, and emphasise the importance of systems instead. Adopting an attitude of 'incredulity towards metanarratives'[16] (where metanarrative stands for universal theory, such as Marxism has always laid claim to be) is, Lyotard tells us in his most famous book, *The Postmodern Condition* (1979), the defining characteristic of the postmodern outlook, which fosters a healthy scepticism about all such cultural ideals as the 'man' of humanism, and also about the exploitative societies which that ideal has helped to engender over the last few centuries in the West.

We might wonder whether this is all just a bit facile, however, and whether tradition and the past can be so easily brushed aside as post-modernists would like to believe. Derrida will prove to be far more circumspect on this issue. We might wonder, too, about the motives of those pressing us so forcefully to reject our past – Fukuyama being a key case in point.

Fukuyama and the End of History

According to Fukuyama, writing in the late 1980s, we have reached the 'end point of mankind's ideological evolution'.[17] This dramatic version of the end of history had a definite vogue in the immediate period after the collapse of communism, capturing, as it seemed so neatly to do, the spirit of the times, when political change was occurring in Eastern Europe with a hitherto inconceivable rapidity to a generation brought up under the sterile cultural certainties of the Cold War. It was at once a triumphalist and an optimistic message. Triumphalist, in that it *did* herald the death of communism; optimistic, in that it celebrated the end of the Cold War, the nuclear arms race that went along with it, and the massive sense of insecurity that these phenomena had induced in a large part of the world's population over a period of several decades. Fukuyama saw general assent for his position when he surveyed the new global political scene, observing that

a remarkable consensus concerning the legitimacy of liberal democracy as a system of government had emerged throughout the world over the past few years, as it conquered rival ideologies like hereditary monarchy, fascism, and most recently communism.[18]

As one might expect, from here it is but a short step to the suggestion that liberal democracy might well be the 'final form of human government'.[19] Communism can come to seem no more than a bad dream that, fortunately enough, we are now able to put behind us.

Fukuyama's claim can be seen as an extension of the 'end of ideology' debate initiated by various American thinkers in the 1950s; most notably, perhaps, by the sociologist Daniel Bell, whose conclusion back in the early 1960s was that 'ideology, which was once a road to action, has come to be a dead end'.[20] Bell was prognosticating from within a Cold War that was still unresolved; but, for Fukuyama, the collapse of communism seemed to provide conclusive proof of the end of ideology as we had known it. To argue the end of ideology is, however, paradoxical as it may seem, still to be ideological, since what is really being called for is the destruction of an *opposing* ideology to one's own – in this instance, the opposition to liberal democracy. It is conventional in such cases to believe that one's opponent has an ideology, but that one's own side does not. Only the *enemy* are nasty ideologues, whereas we stand for the cause of freedom, justice, human rights, etc. From this perspective, liberal democracy is not an ideology so much as an ideal state of affairs, which, as Fukuyama somewhat ingenuously claims, cannot be improved upon. It is rather as if all of world history were to be regarded, in retrospect, as an inevitable progress towards an objective that we have now, thankfully, reached. It is an argument that we live in the best of all possible worlds – and that world is the world of liberal democratic capitalism. Anyone who dissents from this reading of events must be, at best, misguided; at worst, an enemy of humankind with decidedly ulterior motives.

Fukuyama is at pains to point out, after the controversial reception accorded his first piece of writing on the subject (an article in the

American political journal *The National Interest* in 1989), that he is not proclaiming the end of history in any literal sense, 'but History: that is, history understood as a single, coherent, evolutionary process'.[21] Many critics, it is true, did trivialise, and almost deliberately misread, his original idea, hence the careful distinction Fukuyama feels compelled to make. What is being argued for, in other words, is the end of a certain concept of history, which, somewhat surprisingly perhaps, takes Fukuyama quite close to the ideas of those arch-exponents of 'History', Hegel and Marx. In both cases they, too, were proclaiming the end of a certain concept of history, in which, as Fukuyama puts it, 'there would be no further progress in the development of underlying principles and institutions, because all the really big questions had been settled'.[22]

The crucial difference comes in what one thinks is the answer to the 'really big' political questions. For Hegel, it is something like the

Prussian state in which he ended his academic career; for Marx, it is communism and the 'dictatorship of the proletariat'; for Fukuyama, it is the ideal which 'could not be improved upon' – liberal democracy. Fukuyama is already convinced that the free market is the most natural form of economic organisation, arguing that 'the logic of modern natural science would seem to dictate a universal evolution in the direction of capitalism'.[23] His overall concern in *The End of History* is to advance a 'History' that will also end in the triumph of liberal democracy, since it remains his firm belief that 'liberal democracy in reality constitutes the best possible solution to the human problem'.[24] Cultural relativism proves to be yet another candidate for an 'end' to its reign, therefore, with Fukuyama treating it as little more than the consequence of unequal social development, to be overcome by 'a continuing convergence in the types of institutions governing most advanced societies'.[25] Eventually, he argues, we shall all reach the same destination.

If there is a cloud on Fukuyama's horizon, it is the fear that, as the 'last men' of history (the phrase itself is drawn from the work of Nietzsche), we will find life too tame and regress to our old squabbling selves:

The life of the last man is one of physical security and material plenty . . . is the danger that we will be happy on one level, but still dissatisfied with ourselves on another, and hence ready to drag the world back into history with all its wars, injustice, and revolution?[26]

Yet despite such nagging doubts, he is optimistic about humanity's prospects, as well as utterly persuaded that liberal democracy is the only sensible outcome to aim for.

Baudrillard and the End of History

Postmodernist thinkers have been particularly attracted to notions like the end of history.

This is hardly surprising, given that post-modernism is a movement claiming that belief in the old established ways of doing things has irredeemably broken down. To quote a famous phrase by the doyen of postmodern thought, Jean-François Lyotard: 'We no longer have recourse to the grand narratives – we can resort neither to the dialectic of Spirit nor even to the emancipation of humanity as a valida-tion for postmodern scientific discourse.'[27] Science in this case is our passage into the world of the unknown, and tradition can offer little help in such inquiries. The past – particu-larly its grand narratives (that is, universal the-ories) – cannot tell us what the future, the realm of the unpredictable, will turn out to be. Marx, in other words, can no longer be regarded as a prophet dispensing incontestable wisdom. His grand narrative has been tried and found severely wanting, and we have in consequence nothing more to hope from it. Granted, there are things we can learn from the past (history consisting of alternating modernisms and post-modernisms to Lyotard), but we are in no way to consider ourselves as bound by its world-views or conceptions of socio-historical development: goodbye Hegel, goodbye Marx.

Tradition is simply dismissed altogether in Jean Baudrillard's even more radical vision of the end of history. History, to Baudrillard, is the *source* of humankind's problems rather than merely the *site* of them, and in the most cavalier of fashions he calls for history's abolition: 'It is precisely in history that we are alienated, and if we leave history we also leave alienation (not without nostalgia, it must be said, for that good old drama of subject and object).'[28] The solution to political conflict, it would appear, is to become resolutely apolitical; but as Baudrillard's critics have been quick to point out, in practice this amounts to an acceptance of the political status quo. Opting out of political action (which Baudrillard strongly recommends as a mode of existence in several of his later works), at the very least, his critics also observe, makes life considerably easier for those controlling the status quo. Adopting the Baudrillard line would result in much less active opposition to the political establishment's plans, after all. To abolish history is at the same time to abolish the possibility of political change, and Baudrillard is in this respect every bit as guilty as Fukuyama of possessing a disguised ideological agenda.

Lyotard and the End of History

Lyotard's take on the end of history is worth commenting on, given that it is a vision, and a singularly bleak one at that, of both the end of history and the end of the world. *The Inhuman* pictures a world where the forces of techno-science (that is, advanced capitalism) are concerned above all to prolong life past the end of our universe. It will not, however, be life as we currently know it; rather, what is being sought is the ability to make thought possible without the presence of a body. Bodies, under the dispensation of the death of the sun, are to be regarded as a liability. Lyotard proceeds to sketch out a nightmare vision in which computers take over from the human, given that they are less vulnerable and more efficient than human beings – and also, even more crucially from the point of view of techno-scientists, more susceptible to control: 'among the events which the programme attempts to neutralize as much as it can one must, alas, also count the unforseeable effects engendered by the contingency and freedom proper to the human project.'[29] The human body becomes outmoded hardware in such a schema, where it is the software, thought, that is the prized element instead. This is thought, however, divorced from the body where it standardly takes place, and thought under the strict control of a programme concerned with efficiency to the apparent exclusion of all other considerations.

What Lyotard pictures is the dark side to

Baudrillard's alienation-free, post-historical state. There is certainly no history here. As Lyotard acidly remarks: 'Is a computer in any way here and now? Can anything *happen* with it? Can anything happen *to* it?'[30] Neither is there any alienation, merely an endless 'present' with computer programs hyper-efficiently, and bodilessly, going about their allotted tasks minus 'the contingency and freedom proper to the human project'. The end of history, as engineered by the forces of techno-science, looks like a highly undesirable state; an 'inhuman' state, in fact, which Lyotard regards it as our duty to oppose with whatever means come to hand – even though he is somewhat less than sanguine about our ultimate chances of success in the prospective struggle. The techno-scientific project would appear to be the grand narrative to end all grand narratives, with dissent ceasing to be a factor in the absence of the human.

Consciousness and the End of History

Lyotard's vision of science is a particularly negative one, but some commentators can extract a more positive message from the development of our scientific knowledge that might resolve the problem Lyotard is grappling with. Human consciousness is, after all, *part* of the universe, rather than a mere *observer* of it, and in that guise, it has been argued, it may be able to develop to the extent of altering the future physics of that universe – perhaps even to prevent what at the moment appears to be the inescapable death of our sun and home planet. The scientist Paul Davies, for example, has speculated along precisely those lines about the interaction of consciousness and matter:

. . . there is still a sense in which human mind and society may represent only an intermediate stage on the ladder of organizational progress in the cosmos. To borrow a phrase from Louise

Young, the universe is as yet 'unfinished'. We find ourselves living at an epoch only a few billion years after the creation. From what can be deduced about astronomical processes, the universe could remain fit for habitation for trillions of years, possibly for ever.[31]

An unfinished universe still holds out possibilities, and is not necessarily to be regarded as a programme running inexorably and unchangeably through to its predetermined end. Higher levels of organisation (of consciousness, for example) may develop, with the ability to defer that end – without having to cede the field to the computer programs of the techno-scientific establishment. Perhaps the game does not have to be given up by humanity quite yet.

Davies gives us a much more optimistic vision of the future, therefore, in which the end of history need never happen. Yet it does have the drawback, and a very considerable one at that, of being entirely speculative. The vision we are offered goes so far beyond current knowledge and understanding of physical processes, and our place in them, as to seem more like science fiction than science; and that is highly unlikely to quell the disquiet felt about the end of the world and history, as well as the role of advanced capitalistic techno-science in those processes, by anyone in the Lyotard camp. From where we are now standing, the prognosis looks less than favourable.

What's the *Différance*? The Deconstructive Ethos

Derrida's concern with the end of history is, as was argued earlier, entirely consistent with someone committed to the principles of deconstruction. We can now consider what it is about that movement of thought that makes the notion quite so fascinating. Drawing on some previous work I have done on the topic, we might describe the basic assumptions of deconstruction as follows:

(i) that language is ineradicably marked by instability and indeterminacy of meaning;

(ii) that given such instability and indeterminacy, no method of analysis (such as philosophy or criticism) can have any special claim to authority as regards textual interpretation;

(iii) that interpretation is, therefore, a free-ranging activity more akin to game-playing than to analysis as we normally understand that term.[32]

This may make deconstruction sound somewhat frivolous, even marginal to cultural debate (and a legion of commentators has levelled just that accusation against it over the years); but it does have its serious side, in being concerned to make us re-examine the grounds of our own interpretive methods, which often enough will be found to rest on fairly shaky authority – if any at all. Ultimately, deconstruction is to be regarded as a very thoroughgoing form of philosophical scepticism that calls our unexamined assumptions into question, and, at its best, demonstrates where there are gaps in these that render our value judgements more than a little suspect. This may suggest that deconstruction is a predominantly negative form of thought, one largely concerned to show us what *does not* work rather than what does. I hope to show, however, that Derrida's critique of the 'end of history' school does have a very positive side to it – a positive side that leads us straight back into political debate. As the author remarks in *Specters*, 'I believe in the political virtue of the *contretemps*',[33] and there is nothing like a *contretemps* to inspire debate.

Derrida is notorious for insisting that deconstruction has no concepts; nevertheless, he does have his own battery of terms that function much like concepts in standard intellectual discourse, and the most important of these are worth outlining briefly to gain a sense of the deconstructive ethos and its methods. He considers that our use of language is marked by what he calls '*différance*' (a neologism coined by him from the French word *différence*, the latter carrying the meaning of both 'difference' and 'deferral'). The fact that the latter meanings cannot be distinguished in speech, but only in writing, demonstrates for Derrida the inherent instability of meaning, which, as he puts it, is always both 'differed' and 'deferred' (and the words *différance* and *différence* are indistinguishable in speech too). Deconstruction, as a movement of thought, is concerned above all to draw the fact of linguistic instability to our attention. *Différance*, the manifestation of that instability, is to be found, Derrida argues, everywhere in our discourse, serving to disrupt our conventional conception of language as a stable medium for the communication of meaning between individuals.

Another key concept is 'erasure', by means of which Derrida claims that he can use the same terms as his opponents, while denying that they carry the same significance for him, since he is to be considered as using them 'under erasure' (*sous rature*): that is, as if they had a line crossed through them. Another way to think of this method of operation would be to imagine that everything Derrida says is in quotation marks. Critics, not surprisingly, tend to regard this as a form of intellectual cheating, by which Derrida claims not to be bound by the same rules of argument as his opponents – such as the agreed convention that words have fixed meanings that all contributors to a discourse must respect. Erasure has even been turned against him, with one prominent critic, the American Wayne C. Booth, wittily remarking that 'everything I write about Derrida is, like everything he writes, *sous rature*, "under erasure": cross out this footnote'.[34]

Derrida is also concerned to counter what he refers to as the 'metaphysics of presence', the notion that meaning can be grasped in its entirety by language users, that the meanings of words are 'present' to us in our mind when we speak or write them, such that they can be passed on to others in a fairly pure form. For Derrida, this is a mere illusion, if also, as he acknowledges, a very deeply ingrained one in our culture. Discourse in the West is, in fact, *founded* on that illusion. We believe that the meanings of words can be pinned down, and that, as long as we strive for precision in our language use, we can communicate those meanings to others in a relatively unproblematical fashion. Philosophy most certainly works on that principle. To believe in the metaphysics of presence in this way is to be committed to what Derrida calls 'logocentricity' – another of the besetting illusions of Western culture that deconstruction is determined to unmask. For Derrida and his deconstructionist disciples, there are always gaps in communication, and no way that meaning can ever be present in its totality at any one point. Meaning is to be considered, instead, as a process in a constant state of change, never quite all there when a word is used, but always differed from itself, as well as deferred from reaching any sense of completeness.

One of the consequences of Derrida's views on language is that all discourses are seen to depend heavily on rhetoric and the play of language. Philosophy, therefore, has no greater claim to truthfulness than, say, literature, since it is no less subject to the slippage of meaning. As Norris has observed, if taxed on this score by opponents, 'Derrida can always respond by pointing out that philosophy has constantly sustained itself on metaphors, notably those which assimilate truth and reason to the idea of a pure, self-present speech'.[35] Philosophers may well strive for precision of meaning in their arguments, both written and spoken, but they are no more able to achieve this ideal than is any other language user, and the widely-held idea that philosophy can stand as a final court of appeal on questions of meaning and truth-value is, from a deconstructionist perspective, merely another of the illusions that we allow ourselves to be taken in by in Western culture. *All* writing is to be considered as marked by the operation of *différance* (differed from/deferred from), and none can claim to have any greater authority than the rest. The same goes for Derrida's own writing, of course, which might be thought to put something of a question mark over *its* pronouncements as well, although Derrida tends to argue that he is merely describing how language works, rather than pretending to be able to overcome its inherent limitations (an argument which has left many unconvinced, it should be said).

It becomes relatively easy to see why Derrida would object to the idea of the 'end of history', given that it transgresses so many of the principles of deconstruction outlined above. There is the matter of its claiming to be an unproblematical concept, for example, whose meaning cannot be misconstrued (a classic example of reliance on the metaphysics of presence, therefore); of its being able to mark the boundaries of a process, and grasp the totality of that process, as if *différance* (differing/deferring) did not apply; and of assuming, as Fukuyama clearly does, that one is in possession of the authority to render all other interpretations of a particular phenomenon invalid. The world of discourse is infinitely more complex, and certainly far messier, to a deconstructionist than it is to an 'end of history' advocate.

The Politics of Deconstruction

We might well ask why Derrida, an essentially sceptically-minded thinker, would be drawn to Marx, whose work has been turned into something very much akin to a body of unopposable doctrine over the course of the 20th century. Soviet Marxism, for example, adopted a particularly dogmatic attitude to the supposed truth of the canon of Marx's works, to the extent of suppressing, often brutally, even the merest hint of dissent from those in its sphere of influence. Derrida shows himself well aware of the perplexity that his pro-Marxist stance is likely to induce in his audience, especially in the context of the early 1990s: 'Already I hear people saying: "You picked a good time to salute Marx!" Or else: "It's about time!" "Why so late?".'[36] The latter two remarks refer to the fact that Derrida has often implied a left-wing orientation to his thought, and even, on occasion, a qualified support for Marxism. Thus, as long ago as 1971, we find him asserting that 'I am not advocating anything contrary to "Marxism"';[37] (against that, it deserves to be noted that the most sustained study of the relationship between Marxism and deconstruction concluded that 'Derrida is not a marxist philosopher, nor is deconstruction a marxist philosophy'[38]). Derrida's detractors, however, have insisted that, far from providing anything like a blueprint for political action, deconstruction, with its tendency to call into question the ground of authority for nearly everything we say, in reality *inhibits* such action. Arguing that there is both a Marxism of the left and of the right hardly helps matters much, either.

Specters of Marx certainly goes some way towards answering such criticisms as the latter (Marx is praised fulsomely on several occasions, as we shall see), although it does so in Derrida's characteristically oblique and eccentric manner, with a certain amount of 'sophistical doodling' taking place along the way. Derrida is not someone who believes in sudden breaks in cultural processes, or, for that matter, in precise origins to such processes either. As he once pointed out in an interview:

I do not believe in decisive ruptures, in an unequivocal 'epistemological break', as it is called today. Breaks are always, and fatally, reinscribed in an old cloth that must continually, interminably be undone. This interminability is not an accident, or contingency; it is essential, systematic, and theoretical.[39]

Marxism is similarly to be considered as re-inscribed in the 'old cloth' that is history, and in the particular historical conditions that brought it about. It is, in other words, not something we can ever escape from, ignore, or claim finally to have overcome. Instead, it is, to continue Derrida's metaphor, part of the tapestry of our lives. Marxism cannot therefore just suddenly 'end', as so many commentators would gleefully declare that it had when communism imploded in Europe in the 1980s – with the fall of the Berlin Wall singled out as a highly symbolic act in the process of disintegration.

It is, on the other hand, Marx who becomes highly symbolic to Derrida. He cannot be 'edited out' of our cultural heritage. Any attempt to do so will simply cause him to return in the form of a ghost – an interesting image this, since as Derrida points out, the *Communist Manifesto* itself starts out by evoking an image of a ghost: 'A spectre is haunting Europe – the spectre of communism.' Derrida even refers to Marx's 'spectropolitics' and 'genealogy of ghosts'[40] at one point in his argument, to draw attention to what he feels is something of an obsession in the work of the earlier thinker. Communism, it would seem, was a spectre even before it began – precisely the kind of paradox that Derrida delights in dangling before us. The suggestion is that communism is something that will resist expulsion from the Western consciousness, that its message will continue to haunt us, because in a way it always *has* haunted us (it is no accident that Derrida somewhat jauntily refers to his inquiry as a '*hauntology*'[41]). Rather like the ghost in *Hamlet*, an analogy Derrida pursues at some length over the course of this study, the spectre leads us back to the past, making us aware of the seamless nature of history. The conclusion we are supposed to draw is that there is neither a beginning nor an end to Marx's thought – nor to history either. That is what a 'hauntology' will reveal to us.

Nor does Derrida stint in his praise of what that line of thought continues to symbolise for us: 'Upon rereading the *Manifesto* and a few other great works of Marx', he points out, 'I said to myself that I know of few texts in the philosophical tradition, perhaps none, whose lesson seemed more urgent today'.[42] Far from signalling the end of history, Marx opens up debates for us leading *into* the future. Through Marx, and all the 'spectres' that cluster around his name, we can *resist* the end of history – and all those, such as Fukuyama, who would manipulate that concept for their own socio-political advantage. After a career spent frustrating those on the left who would wish to pin him down politically (for or against revolution, or some specific left-wing cause of the day), Derrida finally aligns himself with Marx in late career; but, to the chagrin of the Marxist establishment, such as it now is in a post-communist world, not with the Marx of the classical tradition. Just as Engels reported that Marx himself disclaimed being a Marxist, so Derrida can declare firmly that neither is he ('What is certain is that I am not a Marxist . . . What is the distinguishing trait of a Marxist statement? And who can still say "I am a Marxist"?'[43]); but he continues nevertheless to invoke the spirit of Marx in his critique of liberal democracy.

Spirits, Spectres, and Deferring the End

We might now consider what Derrida means by 'the end of a certain *concept* of history'. It is the concept with which we are all familiar in the West: history as a site of ideological conflict between competing world-systems (liberal democracy versus communism, latterly), each striving to persuade us that it is the more capable of delivering humankind from the twin evils of material want and socio-political oppression. In this respect, both liberal democracy and Marxism are heirs of what has come to be known as the 'Enlightenment project':

that cultural movement in the West that, from the 18th century onwards, has striven to put reason at the centre of human affairs in order to improve mankind's quality of life. That particular concept of history certainly *has* ended in the wake of communism's collapse (as well as the rise of a sceptically-inclined post-modernism), but not, Derrida is insisting, history itself – nor the possibility of yet *other* concepts of history. We cannot exorcise the ghosts of history, and these will continue to haunt us unless we find ways of coming to terms with them – as in the notable case of the 'spectre' of Marx (and the spectre that communism has always been since its inception).

Marx is too deeply ingrained in our cultural heritage to be dismissed, as some of the more radical post-Marxist thinkers would have us believe he can be. Lyotard, for example, exhorts us to expunge Marx and all his works from our lives in a postmodern world: 'We no longer want to correct Marx, to reread him or to read him in the sense that the little Althusserians would like to "read *Capital*": to interpret it according to "its truth". We have no plan to be true, to give the truth of Marx . . .'[44] (The reference is to the French 'structural Marxist' philosopher Louis Althusser, whose reading of Marx emphasised its 'scientific' character above all.) Marx has for Lyotard little more than nuisance value, and is hardly worth engaging with intellectually any longer. The attitude, not infrequently met with in post-modern circles, is one of 'who cares?' For Derrida, on the other hand, Marx remains a cultural figure of considerable consequence, one who still speaks to us very directly today, even in the aftermath of communism's recent demise:

It will always be a fault not to read and reread and discuss Marx – which is to say also a few others – and to go beyond scholarly 'reading' or 'discussion'. It will be more and more a fault, a failing of theoretical, philosophical, political responsibility. When the dogma machine and the 'Marxist' ideological apparatuses (States, parties, cells, unions, and other places of doctrinal production) are in the process of disappearing, we no longer have any excuse, only alibis, for turning away from this responsibility. There will be no future without this. Not without Marx, no future without Marx, without the memory and the inheritance of Marx: in any case of a certain Marx, of his genius, of at least one of his spirits.[45]

It is a case of unweaving the 'old cloth' yet again; not in spite of, but *because* of communism's collapse. There can be no sudden break of the 'Marxism is dead' variety: to believe otherwise is to be philosophically naive. The interminable work of interpretation, that speciality of deconstruction as Derrida repeatedly points out throughout his writings, must go on – and then on and on again. Who cares?

Well, Derrida for one clearly does.

Derrida makes the point that it is possible to be late for this particular version of the end of history, because his generation has been there before (a certain weary air of 'been there, done that' creeps into his narrative at this stage of the proceedings, which younger generations may find a trifle irritating). Marxism, and all that it stands for, may appear to be in terminal crisis in the early 1990s when Derrida is putting together *Specters*, but similar feelings were being expressed back in the author's youth. 'For many of us', he notes, 'a certain (and I emphasise *certain*) end of communist Marxism did not await the recent collapse of the USSR and everything that depends on it throughout the world. All that started – all that was *déjà vu*, indubitably – at the beginning of the 50s'.[46] This is typical Derrida in its identification of networks ('traces', as he would have them) stretching back into the past – before the beginning of the end, as it were. A sense of *déjà vu* already applies at the 'origin' of Marxism's decline, because that decline has its source in the yet deeper past. Perhaps it was even present in Marx himself, hence that 'spectre' of communism he feels compelled to invoke in the *Manifesto*? Not only can one be late for the end of history, one cannot prevent oneself from being late for its beginning either. The end is always deferred in one direction, while the beginning always turns out to be before wherever one happens to start from in the other direction.

The passage is typical Derrida, too, in its language play, this being an activity that deconstruction makes very much its own. The emphasis on the word 'certain' leaves us no wiser as to whether Derrida means 'certain' as in 'definite' ('certain to happen', for example), or 'certain' as in 'particular version of' ('a certain aspect'). Derrida being Derrida, he almost undoubtedly means both simultaneously. Given the instability of language, one is always too late for the full meaning of words as well, it would seem. Like the end of history, meaning is always being deferred (and Derrida will also make great play throughout *Specters* of the double meaning of the word 'spirit', as both 'consistent with the ideals of' – 'in the spirit of' – and 'spectre'). It is in the nature of decon-struction not just to see the wider context (those traces, or spectres, stretching back into the past in an infinite regress), but also the fluidity, the flexibility, the ultimately uncon-trollable nature of that context. One cannot, successfully anyway, police meaning or history; nor can one offer complete interpretations of them. Deconstruction is a warning against human presumption in this regard. A warning that the totality of *any* large-scale phenomenon, such as meaning and history, will always man-age somehow to elude us. To claim otherwise is to be, in a literal sense, 'totalitarian', and Derrida is quite happy elsewhere in his work to play on the authoritarian political overtones which that term inevitably carries, especially in the aftermath of such notorious 20th-century figures as Stalin or Mao.

If scarcely in the Stalin or Mao class, Fukuyama nevertheless stands indicted on this score too: that is, guilty of trying to exclude other interpretations of historical phenomena than his own (cultural relativism being excluded from the agenda in his case, as we have seen). Derrida, on the other hand, is trying to keep the debate open; and from this perspective, deconstruction, so often accused by its critics of being an apolitical movement of thought, has a very definite political edge to it indeed.

The Ideal and the Real: Demolishing Fukuyama

That political edge is at its keenest when Derrida directly addresses the arguments put forward by Fukuyama in *The End of History*. In the *Specters* essay 'Conjuring – Marxism', for example, Derrida sets about demolishing

Fukuyama's book with some gusto, accusing it of numerous failings, ranging from philosophical *naïveté* to bad faith (with a large dose of pseudo-evangelism thrown in for good measure). The major criticism turns out to be that Fukuyama glosses over the discrepancy between the ideal and the real as regards liberal democracy. Thus we find him blithely remarking in *The End of History*'s introduction: 'While some present-day countries might fail to achieve stable liberal democracy, and others might lapse back into other, more primitive forms of rule like theocracy or military dictatorship, the *ideal* of liberal democracy could not be improved on.'[47] One might well wonder why the ideal is having quite such difficulty establishing itself if it is so self-evidently superior to all other forms of socio-political organisation, and whether that difficulty perhaps points to some structural flaws within liberal democratic ideology itself (Fukuyama puts the blame on unequal social development and residual human perversity instead). Derrida is not slow to make such a point, arguing that the reality of liberal democracy is little more than a travesty of its ideals – even if one accepted those ideals, which Derrida makes plain he does not:

It would be too easy to show that, measured by the failure to establish liberal democracy, the gap between fact and ideal essence does not show up only in these so-called primitive forms of government, theocracy, and military dictatorship ... this failure and gap also characterize, a priori *and by definition, all democracies, including the oldest and most stable of so-called Western democracies.*[48]

Derrida is in his element in such cases. Pointing out gaps in systems of thought has always been one of the major preoccupations of deconstruction – as it invariably is in all forms of philosophical scepticism.

Fukuyama stands accused by Derrida of a major misreading of the contemporary global political situation. Where the former sees at the very least tacit acceptance of the liberal democratic ideal, and a tide running strongly in its favour (that 'remarkable consensus' he announces so confidently in the early stages of *The End of History*), the latter sees instead an ideology in a virtual state of siege, asking, with more than a hint of asperity, 'is it still necessary to point out that liberal democracy of the par-liamentary form has never been so much in the minority and so isolated in the world? That it has never been in such a state of dysfunction in what we call the Western democracies?'[49] It takes far more than unequal social develop-ment and residual human perversity to explain the reasons for this state of affairs to Derrida's satisfaction, and he proceeds to itemise the fail-ings of liberal democracy as he perceives them, producing a catalogue running from mass unemployment and the plight of the homeless, through to the machinations of the arms industry and the manipulation of the United Nations (and most other international institutions, for that matter), by the Western superpowers. It is a catalogue that, in his eyes, demolishes any pretensions Fukuyama may have to occupy the moral high ground:

For it must be cried out, at a time when some have the audacity to neo-evangelize in the name of the ideal of a liberal democracy that has finally realized itself as the ideal of human history: never have violence, inequality, exclusion, famine, and thus economic oppression affected as many human beings in the history of the earth and of humanity.[50]

By Derrida's standards, this is unusually explicit political rhetoric, and he follows it up with a call for the construction of a 'New International' of left-wing interests to continue the fight against injustice that had spurred Marx on to the composition of his major works.

What Derrida is seeking is 'a link of affinity, suffering, and hope'[51] that leads back to Marx and his concerns, even if it does so in a manner calculated to irritate most present-day Marxists by an insistence on the spirit rather than the letter of Marx's cultural critique. Derrida is unworried by such a prospect, feeling that he is keeping faith with the original, self-critical, spirit of Marxism (while continuing to play on the double meaning of that word 'spirit'), and feeling also that one cannot just dispense with this spirit as Fukuyama believes is possible after communism's European demise. In Derrida's reading of history, Marx will not go that quietly: 'Whether they wish it or know it or not, all men and women, all over the earth, are today to a certain extent the heirs of Marx and Marxism . . . we cannot not be its heirs.'[52] Both the spirit and the spectre of Marx remain, whatever pro-nouncements Fukuyama and his followers may make about communism's political eclipse. Far from presiding over the end of history, we are seemingly better placed than ever to destabilise the liberal democratic ideal that blinds so many to the real state of affairs in the world around us. Where Fukuyama finds 'good news' to report, Derrida's vision of our current socio-political condition is altogether grimmer, and he is particularly scathing of the evangelical cast to Fukuyama's thought, with its echoes of the fundamentalist Christian right in American politics.

Even though it is difficult to specify very precisely what the planned 'New International' will actually *do* to rectify the situation, other than proselytise in the manner of *Specters*, it represents, nevertheless, a ringing endorsement of the continuing political relevance of the Marxist message – spectres and all.

A Question for Today?

So the answer is, yes, this is very much a question for today, since it asks us to confront a strain of triumphalism within Western culture that is ideologically highly suspect. Derrida is right to remind us that history does not end, or cannot be brought to an end by the mere fiat of any self-interested ideologue, whereas concepts of history patently do. That realisation invites us to scrutinise the ideology that lies behind our concept of history – including, crucially, the ideology of the end of history, with its overtones not just of triumphalism, but of intolerance towards ways of life other than one's own. It becomes a question of what the end of history, especially in its Fukuyama-style manifestation of 'continuing convergence' of interests, excludes.

One possible answer to that question is *dissent*. This is a point forcefully raised by the sociologist Zygmunt Bauman, who, though no apologist for communism, nonetheless regrets the impact that the collapse of communism has had on the political life of the West. Bauman bemoans the lack of an ideological opposite to

Western liberal democracy, an opposite that, in the still recent past of the Cold War period, helped to keep capitalism relatively honest in its dealings with the citizens of Western societies. Our current condition, on the other hand, he refers to as 'living without an alternative'.[53] Capitalism triumphant is, in Bauman's opinion, capitalism dangerously rampant and unchecked, and with almost unlimited power and authority to exploit and control the lives of defenceless individuals – especially individuals with no alternative whatsoever to turn to in the political lives of their own countries. Western society, Bauman points out, now 'has neither effective enemies inside nor barbarians knocking at the gates, only adulators and imitators. It has practically (and apparently irrevocably) de-legitimized all alternatives to itself'.[54] Derrida's spirit of Marx, with its appeal to plural – as well as pluralist-minded – socio-political constituencies, is designed to counter precisely that triumphalism, with all the drawbacks that accompany it, and thus constitutes a radical answer to a vexed question.

Seen from this Bauman-Derrida perspective, one can, indeed one *should*, be late to the end of history, since that demonstrates resistance to an authoritarianism that is all too typically a stock-in-trade of ideology in general. And if there is one thing that postmodern thinkers of all persuasions are agreed upon, it is that they despise authoritarianism in whatever form it may take. Ideology controls individuals all the more effectively where all alternatives to itself are, as Bauman puts it, 'de-legitimized'. That is why the spirit of Marx is worth keeping alive. Derrida invites us, in other words, to be sceptical of political authority, and to build a 'New International' to that effect. In a Western society that is currently 'living without an alternative', and where political dissent in consequence can come to seem mere perversity for its own sake, that is an offer we *can* understand – and, I would wish to argue, one by which we can also profit. Being late for the end of history is to be considered a politically radical act where the end of history is seen to equal the end of political debate.

One can, however, point to a residual problem that Derrida's analysis bequeaths to the left. It is that, using the same principles of argument put forward by Derrida, one could also prove that liberal democracy and capitalism cannot just 'end' either. Think, for example, of how capitalism so rapidly re-emerged in the old Soviet bloc after the end of decades of communist rule (over 70 years in Russia's case), rather as if *its* spectre had never been exorcised properly either. Derrida argues that when capitalist societies try to deny the historical fact of communism, or dismiss it as a mere ghost, 'They do no more than disavow the undeniable itself: a ghost never dies, it remains always to come and to come-back'.[55] Yet, equally, one must assume that the ghost of capitalism also 'remains always to come and to come-back' whenever socialism is in the ascendant. Maybe the only thing that Derrida's argument proves is that spectres are permanent factors in our lives, whatever the current political dispensation may happen to be – hence the need for a 'hauntology' to enable us to reach some kind of accommodation with them: 'they are always *there*, specters, even if they do not exist, even if they are no longer, even if they are not yet'.[56] It is back to the idea of the 'old cloth that must continually, interminably be undone'; that is, back to interpretation, revision of one's theories, and the duty of undertaking cultural analysis that we have inherited from such figures as Marx. Fukuyama's fault is that he sees an end to those processes, rather than a summons to re-engage in debate.

What Derrida is *not* providing, it should be noted, is any basis for triumphalism on the left. *Specters* is no mere mirror-image of Fukuyama, as Derrida's pronouncement that 'the dead can often be more powerful than the living'[57] emphatically signals to us. Spectropolitics, so the message would seem to go, is always with us. Whether as benign spirits or frightening spectres, or, most likely, some uneasy combination of the two that we find hard to disentangle, those dead will continue to haunt us and to defer the possibility of any end to history. As heirs to the past, and Derrida insists this is a role that we are not at liberty to refuse ('we cannot not be its heirs'), we have no option but to extend history, and the spectropolitical project that invariably accompanies it, into the indefinite future. The 'end of history' is not the good news that Fukuyama believes it to be; not if we have any desire at all to contest the balance of economic and political power that currently prevails in our world. It may have taken a while to establish it with certainty, and kept many in suspense in the interim, but, ultimately, Derridean deconstruction is on the side of the left-wing angels.

Notes

1. Jacques Derrida, *Specters of Marx: The State of the Debt, the Work of Mourning, and the New International*, trans. Peggy Kamuf, New York and London: Routledge, 1994, p. 15.

2. Arthur Marwick, *The Nature of History*, London and Basingstoke: Macmillan, 1970, p. 13.

3. Derrida, *Specters*, p. 13.

4. Jacques Derrida, *Ear of the Other. Otobiography, Transference, Translation*, trans. Peggy Kamuf, ed. Christie McDonald, Lincoln, NA and London: University of Nebraska Press, 1988, p. 32.

5. Francis Fukuyama, *The End of History and the Last Man*, London: Hamish Hamilton, 1992, pp. xiii, xi.

6. Derrida, *Specters*, p. 68.

7. Bernd Magnus and Stephen Cullenberg, 'Editors' Introduction' to Derrida, *Specters*, pp. vii, viii.

8. The colloquium also produced the companion volume of essays, Bernd Magnus and Stephen Cullenberg, eds., *Whither Marxism?: Global Crises in International Perspective*, New York and London: Routledge, 1995.

9. Derrida, *Specters*, p. 15.

10. Christopher Norris, *Derrida*, London: Fontana, 1987, p. 79.

11. Wayne C. Booth, *Critical Understanding: The Powers and Limits of Pluralism*, Chicago and London: University of Chicago Press, 1979, p. 216.

12. Derrida, *Specters*, p. 15.

13. Jean-François Lyotard, *The Inhuman: Reflections on Time*, trans. Geoffrey Bennington and Rachel Bowlby, Oxford: Basil Blackwell, 1991, pp. 8–9.

14. Michel Foucault, *The Order of Things: An Archaeology of the Human Sciences*, trans. Alan Sheridan-Smith, New York: Random House, 1970, p. 387.

15. Ibid.

16. Jean-François Lyotard, *The Postmodern Condition: A Report on Knowledge*, trans. Geoffrey Bennington and Brian Massumi, Manchester: Manchester University Press, 1984, p. xxiv.

17. Francis Fukuyama, 'The End of History?', *The National Interest*, 16 (1989), pp. 3–18.

18. Fukuyama, *The End of History*, p. xi.

19. Fukuyama, 'The End of History?', pp. 3–18.

20. Daniel Bell, *The End of Ideology: On the Exhaustion of Political Ideas in the Fifties*, New York: Free Press, 1962, p. 393.

21. Fukuyama, *The End of History*, p. xii.

22. Ibid.

23. Ibid., p. xv.

24. Ibid., p. 338.

25. Ibid.

26. Ibid., p. 312.

27. Lyotard, *The Postmodern Condition*, p. 60.

28. Jean Baudrillard, 'The Year 2000 Will Not Take Place', trans. Paul Foss and Paul Patton, in E. A. Grosz et al, eds., *Futur*Fall: Excursions into Post-Modernity*, Sydney: Power Institute of Fine Arts, University of Sydney, 1986, p. 23.

29. Lyotard, *The Inhuman*, p. 69.

30. Ibid., p. 118.

31. Paul Davies, *The Cosmic Blueprint: Order and Complexity at the Edge of Chaos*, Harmondsworth: Penguin, 1995, p. 196.

32. Adapted from the definition of deconstructionist aesthetics given in Stuart Sim, 'Structuralism and Post-Structuralism', in Oswald Hanfling, ed., *Philosophical Aesthetics: An Introduction*, Oxford: Basil Blackwell, 1992, pp. 405–39 (p. 425).

33. Derrida, *Specters*, p. 88.

34. Booth, *Critical Understanding*, p. 367.

35. Norris, *Derrida*, p. 79.

36. Derrida, *Specters*, p. 88.

37. Jacques Derrida, *Positions*, trans. Alan Bass, London: Athlone Press, 1981, p. 63.

38. Michael Ryan, *Marxism and Deconstruction: A Critical Articulation*, Baltimore and London: Johns Hopkins University Press, 1982, p. 9.

39. Derrida, *Positions*, p. 24.

40. Derrida, *Specters*, p. 107.

41. Ibid., p. 10.

42. Ibid., p. 13.

43. Ibid., p. 88.

44. Jean-François Lyotard, *Libidinal Economy*, trans. Iain Hamilton Grant, London: Athlone Press, 1993, p. 96.

45. Derrida, *Specters*, p. 13.

46. Ibid., p. 14.

47. Fukuyama, *The End of History*, p. xi.

48. Derrida, *Specters*, p. 64.

49. Ibid., pp. 78–9.

50. Ibid., p. 85.

51. Ibid.

52. Ibid., p. 91.

53. See chapter 8, 'Living without an Alternative', of Zygmunt Bauman, *Intimations of Postmodernity*, London: Routledge, 1992.

54. Ibid., p. 183.

55. Derrida, *Specters*, p. 99.

56. Ibid., p. 176.

57. Ibid., p. 48.

Bibliography

Bauman, Zygmunt, *Intimations of Postmodernity*, London: Routledge, 1992.

Bell, Daniel, *The End of Ideology: On the Exhaustion of Political Ideas in the Fifties*, New York: Free Press, 1962.

Booth, Wayne C., *Critical Understanding: The Powers and Limits of Pluralism*, Chicago and London: University of Chicago Press, 1979.

Davies, Paul, *The Cosmic Blueprint: Order and Complexity at the Edge of Chaos*, Harmondsworth: Penguin, 1995.

Derrida, Jacques, *Ear of the Other. Otobiography, Transference, Translation*, trans. Peggy Kamuf, ed. Christie McDonald, Lincoln, NA and London: University of Nebraska Press, 1988.

— *Positions*, trans. Alan Bass, London: Athlone Press, 1981.

— *Specters of Marx: The State of the Debt, the Work of Mourning, and the New International*, trans. Peggy Kamuf, New York and London: Routledge, 1994.

Foucault, Michel, *The Order of Things: An Archaeology of the Human Sciences*, trans. Alan Sheridan-Smith, New York: Random House, 1970.

Fukuyama, Francis, 'The End of History?', *The*

National Interest, 16 (1989), pp. 3–18.

— *The End of History and the Last Man*, London: Hamish Hamilton, 1992.

Grosz, E. A., et al, eds., *Futur*Fall: Excursions into Post-Modernity*, Sydney: Power Institute of Fine Arts, University of Sydney, 1986.

Hanfling, Oswald, ed., *Philosophical Aesthetics: An Introduction*, Oxford: Basil Blackwell, 1992.

Lyotard, Jean-François, *The Inhuman: Reflections on Time*, trans. Geoffrey Bennington and Rachel Bowlby, Oxford: Basil Blackwell, 1991.

— *Libidinal Economy*, trans. Iain Hamilton Grant, London: Athlone Press, 1993.

— *The Postmodern Condition: A Report on Knowledge*, trans. Geoffrey Bennington and Brian Massumi, Manchester: Manchester University Press, 1984.

Magnus, Bernd, and Cullenberg, Stephen, eds., *Whither Marxism?: Global Crises in International Perspective*, New York and London: Routledge, 1995.

Marwick, Arthur, *The Nature of History*, London and Basingstoke: Macmillan, 1970.

Norris, Christopher, *Derrida*, London: Fontana, 1987.

Ryan, Michael, *Marxism and Deconstruction: A Critical Articulation*, Baltimore and London: Johns Hopkins University Press, 1982.

Key Ideas

Anthropic Principle

There is an underlying 'anthropic principle' in the view expressed by the scientist Paul Davies on the interaction of consciousness and matter (see pp. 28–30). This is the belief that the laws of physics are such as to promote the development of complex self-organising structures (such as human consciousness). Scientists like Davies find an element of predestiny in the operation of the principle, whereby complex structures are actively encouraged to appear after a certain stage of development; although Davies is careful to point out that this does not mean that their actual form is in any way *predetermined*. It is more the case that, given the right conditions, complex self-organisation will occur. The so-called 'strong anthropic principle' is the belief that the universe organises itself in such a way as to reach a state of self-awareness. According to some scientists, we are in an 'unfinished' universe with the potential for even more complex levels of self-organisation to develop, in which case our fears about the universe ending at some point may prove to be unfounded.

Deconstruction

For Jacques Derrida, deconstruction is not so much a

system of thought as a tactical exercise designed to demonstrate the instability of language and the shaky foundations on which most of our theories rest. Developing the observation made by the Swiss linguist Ferdinand de Saussure that the connection between signifier and signified (that is, word and meaning) is arbitrary, Derrida has devised various methods to draw this arbitrariness to our attention. Word-play and punning, for example, have been tactically deployed by deconstructionist thinkers to show how words are never fixed in their meaning, and are instead always hinting at other contexts than the one they are appearing in. Since discourse in the West is founded on just such a belief in fixed meaning, Derrida's claims have the potential to undermine some of our deepest-held cultural assumptions.

Epistemological Break

The term used by the French philosopher Louis Althusser to describe the difference between Marx's early and mature works. The break takes place in the 1840s, and marks the division between Marx as a conventional philosopher (heavily under the influence of Hegel) and Marx as a 'scientist' of society. Post-break, Marxist theory becomes a scientific instrument for the dissection of a society's ideology. Marxism itself is seen to have moved beyond ideology, and, as a science, to be the source of 'truths' rather than mere interpretations. Marx's own famous aphorism that 'philosophers have only interpreted the world in various ways, the point is, to change it', sums up the difference in attitude between the two phases of his career quite neatly.

History (with a purpose)

Francis Fukuyama's argument in *The End of History and the Last Man* is directed against what we might call 'history with a purpose' – that is, history seen as the realisation of some grand metaphysical scheme, such as Hegel or Marx propound. For Hegel, history was the process through which the 'World Spirit' realised itself. Marx saw history as a class struggle destined to end in the 'dictatorship of the proletariat'. For Fukuyama, the commitment to history with a purpose has led to most of humankind's problems (wars, bloody revolutions, etc.), and we have been given the opportunity, in the aftermath of the collapse of the Soviet Empire, to overcome this obsession and to settle down into a peaceful, liberal democratic lifestyle.

Humanism

Humanism is often a term of abuse in recent cultural debate, with many French theorists in particular espousing an openly *anti*-humanist creed. Our modern conception of the term dates from the Renaissance period. Rooted in the study of classical Greek and Roman culture, Renaissance humanism made 'man' the centre of human concern and encouraged individuals to realise their talents, mental and physical, to the full. Respect for the individual lies at the heart of humanist thought, and it is still an influential doctrine. For many thinkers nowadays, however, humanism is tied up with a particular kind of Western cultural imperialism, where individual entrepreneurialism and market-oriented competition dominate human affairs to the detriment of most of us.

Ideology

In the broadest sense, an ideology is a system of belief by which a society organises itself. One of the most influential concepts of ideology in the 20th century comes from Louis Althusser, for whom it represented a system of belief that attempted to disguise its internal contradictions. Liberal democracy may proclaim that we live in a free-market society where all can compete on equal terms, but in reality the market is an exploitative system rigged in favour of those with the most economic power in society. Lack of success, however, is put down to *individual* failure, rather than the contradictions of the economic system itself. Seen from this perspective, ideology is something that is imposed on us by the ruling élite.

Last Men

In Nietzsche, the 'last men' are those who come before the development of the 'overmen' (often translated as 'supermen'). Last men are despised by Nietzsche for their lack of daring compared to the 'overmen', being intellectually narrow and complacent in outlook. Francis Fukuyama takes over the concept in order to describe his fear that some elements of humanity may choose to resist what for him is the welcome 'end of history'. In the West, we have reached a state of material security which those brought up under old-style 'history with a purpose' may find somewhat unexciting. These 'last men' of a particular line of social development might well become bored enough to try to resuscitate 'history with a purpose' – even in the face of all evidence that it is contrary to humankind's best interests.

Logocentrism

The belief that words can communicate fixed meanings between individuals in a relatively unproblematical fashion. For Jacques Derrida, this is one of the founding assumptions of Western culture, and one that his philosophical method, deconstruction, is designed to call into question. Logocentrism is based on the premise that the full meaning of a word is 'present' to us, in our minds, prior to its communication to others. Derrida dubs this belief 'the metaphysics of presence', and considers it one of the great illusions of Western thought.

Metanarrative

Also referred to as 'grand narrative', this is Jean-François Lyotard's term for a universal theory, such as Marxism or Hegelianism. Such theories claim to be able to offer an explanation for all phenomena, and to make them fit into their system – or 'narrative', as Lyotard would have it. Marxism, for example, sees all human history as the history of class struggle, thus subordinating all other narratives, such as the gender or race ones, to this overriding consideration. In *The Postmodern Condition*, Lyotard argues that all metanarratives have now lost their credibility, and that the appropriate response to adopt in a postmodern world is one of 'incredulity'. The Marxist metanarrative is no longer to be the subject of debate, but simply disbelieved and then ignored.

Modern

'Modern' has come to describe the kind of society that has developed in the West over the last few centuries: one committed to material progress and technological innovation. The overall goal is an improvement in living standards, both in qualitative and quantitative terms; more personal freedom and control over one's environment; more, and better, consumer goods. Modern societies tend to regard nature as something to be exploited and brought under human control as much as possible. They also tend especially to prize innovation and entrepreneurial spirit – traits that can even be found in activities such as the arts. Modern art made something of a fetish out of originality and the notion that the artist had to be constantly challenging existing norms, pushing back the boundaries of the known, etc.

Postmodern

For Jean-François Lyotard, the postmodern condition is that in which we stop believing in the 'meta-narratives' of history, and concentrate our attention on the development of new 'knowledges' that help to break the power of such narratives. Marxism was one such narrative, modernity another. Modern societies, with their commitment to rising living standards and technological innovation, were to be seen as based on a metanarrative of human progress that closed off other possible ways of life ('little narratives', in Lyotard's scheme). Many now dissent from what modernity represented, arguing that it has become an authoritarian system that oppresses the individual. The Greens point out that our obsession with techno-logical progress has despoiled the planet, and perhaps even put our survival as a species at risk. In the political realm, the collapse of Marxism as a global political force represents a victory for the postmodern over the modern, given that Marxism is indelibly associated with the modernist notion of human progress to overcome the deficiencies of class-based societies.

Structural Marxism

Louis Althusser was the moving spirit behind this highly influential hybrid of structuralist and Marxist thought. Structural Marxism took over structuralism's overriding concern with sign systems and their internal grammar, and applied this to the study of 'social formations'. The latter were read as sign systems designed to control us as individuals, and were made up of two main types of institution: the Repressive State Apparatus (RSA) and the Ideological State Apparatus (ISA). Whereas the former (the police force, the army) kept control by threat of violence, the latter (the media, the education system, the arts, etc.) worked more subtly at the level of thought, presenting certain ideologically-approved models for us to emulate. By means of these institutions, individuals were prevented from realising the truth about the ideology that oppressed them. Althusser's detractors have argued that the theory largely excludes the human dimension, giving us 'history without a subject'.

Other titles available in the Postmodern Encounters series from Icon/Totem

Nietzsche and Postmodernism
Dave Robinson
ISBN 1 84046 093 8
UK £2.99   USA $7.95

Friedrich Nietzsche (1844–1900) has exerted a huge influence on 20th century philosophy and literature – an influence that looks set to continue into the 21st century. Nietzsche questioned what it means for us to live in our modern world. He was an 'anti-philosopher' who expressed grave reservations about the reliability and extent of human knowledge. His radical scepticism disturbs our deepest-held beliefs and values. For these reasons, Nietzsche casts a 'long shadow' on the complex cultural and philosophical phenomenon we now call 'postmodernism'.

Nietzsche and Postmodernism explains the key ideas of this 'Anti-Christ' philosopher. It then provides a clear account of the central themes of postmodernist thought exemplified by such thinkers as Derrida, Foucault, Lyotard and Rorty, and concludes by asking if Nietzsche can justifiably be called the first great postmodernist.

Foucault and Queer Theory
Tamsin Spargo
ISBN 1 84046 092 X
UK £2.99   USA $7.95

Michel Foucault is the most gossiped-about celebrity
of French poststructuralist theory. The homophobic
insult 'queer' is now proudly reclaimed by some who
once called themselves lesbian or gay. What is the
connection between the two? This is a postmodern
encounter between Foucault's theories of sexuality,
power and discourse and the current key exponents
of queer thinking who have adopted, revised and
criticised Foucault. Our understanding of gender,
identity, sexuality and cultural politics will be radically
altered in this meeting of transgressive figures.

Baudrillard and the Millennium
Christopher Horrocks
ISBN 1 84046 091 1
UK £2.99   USA $7.95

'In a sense, we do not believe in the Year 2000', says
French thinker Jean Baudrillard. Still more disturbing
is his claim that the millennium might not take place.
Baudrillard's analysis of 'Y2K' reveals a repentant
culture intent on mourning and laundering its past.
Baudrillard and the Millennium confronts the strategies
of this major cultural analyst's encounter with the
greatest non-event of the postmodern age. Key topics,
such as natural catastrophes, the body, 'victim culture',
identity and Internet viruses, are discussed in reference
to the development of Jean Baudrillard's millenarian
thought from the 1980s to the threshold of the Year 2000
– from simulation to disappearance.

Einstein and the Total Eclipse
Peter Coles
ISBN 1 84046 089 X
UK £2.99   USA $7.95

In ancient times, the duration of a total solar eclipse was a time of fear and wonder. The scientific revolution that began with Copernicus relegated these eclipses to the category of 'understood' phenomena. Astronomers still relish their occurrence, not because of the event itself, but because of the opportunity it provides to carry out observations that would otherwise be impossible by day.

This book is about a famous example of this opportunism: the two expeditions to observe the bending of starlight by the Sun – predicted by Einstein's general theory of relativity – from Sobral in northern Brazil and the island of Principe in the Gulf of Guinea during the eclipse of 29 May 1919.

As well as providing a simple way of understanding the key ideas of Einstein's theory, this story offers fascinating insights into the sociological conflicts between 'Big Science' and popular culture that are as real today as they were 80 years ago.